Study in Tango

New York City, July, 2002

Carter Brey

Two Tangos for Solo Cello

I. Tango para Ilaria

II. Study in Tango

EXCLUSIVELY DISTRIBUTED BY

EDWARD B. MARKS MUSIC COMPANY

HAL•LEONARD® CORPORATION

7777 W. BLUEMOUND RD. P.O. BOX 13819 MILWAUKEE, WI 53213

www.ebmarks.com
www.halleonard.com

Study in Tango
for solo cello

CARTER BREY

Tango para Ilaria

plaintive and very free

da capo al segno

Coda

calando

p

ff

savage and heavily accented

ff

Buenos Aires, June, 1997

Tango para Ilaria
for solo cello

CARTER BREY

Study in Tango

U.S. $12.95

HL00120275

ISBN 978-1-4803-4607-9